WATCHNIGHT

WATCHNIGHT

Cyrée Jarelle Johnson

Nightboat Books
New York

Copyright © 2024 Cyrée Jarelle Johnson

Printed in the United States

ISBN: 978-164362-194-4

Cover photo: "Howard Wilson operating the sewing machine in the C. & E. Shoe Shop at Fort Benning, Georgia, as he finishes off a pair of parachutist's boots." July 1942. Collection of the National Archives at College Park.

Cover design by Kit Schluter
Design and typesetting by HR Hegnauer
Typeset in Baskerville and Elequent Pro

Cataloging-in-publication data is available from the Library of Congress

Nightboat Books
New York
www.nightboat.org

Rose. Dear Rose Dear.

    —*Jazz*, Toni Morrison

"The Destiny of Earthseed is to take root among the stars," I said. "That's the ultimate Earthseed aim, and the ultimate human change short of death. It's a destiny we'd better pursue if we hope to be anything other than smooth-skinned dinosaurs—here today, gone tomorrow, our bones mixed with the bones and ashes of our cities, and so what?"

    —*Parable of the Sower*, Octavia Butler

Requiem

What song to sing in tired times as now
when new sprung shoots are crushed beneath the heels
of time, before they grow? Blossom snipped low
by fate's callous blade. How that sorrow feels

like opening to the pain of the world.
Wholed by a light at the snuff of your day,
the end to a story impeccably told.
Though now we must trudge an opposite way

stay close to us. The ones we love who've gone
on to glory, or horror, or nothing—all
linked, ever in memory. Names etched in bone,
or page, or slates of stone on graveyard sprawl.

Yes, grief is a sored horse that bucks and hurts,
yet we tug the reins and survive the worst.

WATCHNIGHT

Now Let the Weeping Cease

After Jericho Brown
After Sophocles

On this land, the weeping time never ceased.
The river is safer than the shore.

The river is safer than the shore
and death is more than a shade who hums back.

My death is a shade that hums back at me.
My ghost hums back across time's night-vast gap.

Even the thought of a ghost bends time.
In which year is today situated?

Our situation is a spectral year,
a year dreamed as though it were a future.

A future soft as a child's daydreams.
My childhood daydreams did not feature me.

I could not picture a featured future.
Now I cast shadows with shades and the night.

Watchnight

I love y'all even if you
get on my whole ass nerves.
(But who doesn't
get on my whole ass nerves?)
Who can get on my whole ass
nerves like you?
And who else would I want to? Pass
that macaroni and cheese
and tell me where the party at.
I don't care what they play as long as we get
some play. Ok, but why your girl put her hand
in the bacon I cooked for the peas?
Didn't even wash 'em
with her no home trainin' ass.
And y'all wonder why
I'm like this. This your company.
Tell your company
that tight blunt is what saved her fingers.
That ain't cute.
Where? Who gone be there?
How much the Uber?
You know I wanna shake my ass
at the after hours
so we can't stay at the queer party.
Nothin' to write home about.
The music didn't even have words.
I need to sing tonight, something I know.
I'm crossfaded and I'm bouta get mean.
Did you put the other half away for morning?

Eating the Other

After bell hooks

> "Master . . . eated me when I was meat"
> —Vincent Woodard, from *The Delectable Negro*

Nat Turner's body is long devoured,
as were mummies and unfortunate men.
I'm sure some slave masters ate their own kin
—caught them off guard, lept up, overpowered

them with a group like some fucking cowards.
They tasted human blood. They killed again.
At the sight of black flesh they eased a grin.
They interred the scraps beneath the flowers

that brightened the plantation door. A horror,
yet also a treat. A slave turned to meat.
If your ship spears no whale choose a martyr,
claim delusion, inhale all you can eat.

The perverse race record never falters:
As you wish, it reads, *but don't waste the feet.*

Cadillac

Those dragged along earth's spine to Savannah
glided back home, miraculous in flight—
rose from the auction block, sweet falsetto
a howl that split a gold road through red sun
that would never open their backs. Perhaps
my ancestor lost her dance steps into the air.

Oh well. Sometimes it be like that. *The air*
too hot to ride, she says. Yet Savannah
slid below the bodies of friends, perhaps
the women she slept near—but they could fly.
Lacking any reasonable plan, sun
glowering towards her with pinched lips, a falsetto

voice walking from the kitchen, falsetto
through gap teeth, not stealing, sucking the air
forced through her mouth's pinprick, haloed by sun
glow that swole her life to ruins. Savannah
sold her child from under her skirts. To fly
seemed the pride of a kicked dream, but perhaps

there is something to want even here, perhaps
love or sex or god. Her man: falsetto
in the woods church. She likes that. Still, can't fly.
Heartbreak Day to gulf or grave, not the air
around her that hovers, spits Savannah
at her as her back bends. Low the red sun

with lips to her neck. Generations sun
glow grew into gold, into rain—perhaps
down the windows of cars to Savannah.
A cadillac—breaks never falsetto,
always shine like buffed leather, cheat the air
of ego. Lifting up to pilfered flight.

Our lives better than death, but worse than flight.
A tan stolen from milder Northern suns,
but breath still beaten out our lungs. The air
too weak to hold us, still. We think perhaps
this year will change hope to fact. Falsetto
cry out pews from Philly to Savannah.

The coastal birds at falsetto pitch fly
to mock us but, perhaps, the reborn sun
o'er Savannah will lift us to the air.

The Wall

A legacy
is a deed
of sale
on the wall
of a New
Jersey administrative
building broom
closet. The only
proof molding above
an open drain.
A country
of round mouths.
Bleached eyes.
Empty fences.
Blank books
& two
(at least)
great swamps.
My swamp:
misunderstood
by land
confounded
by line,
latitude, location
and still
won't tell
me whose
milk filled
my mouth.

Ugly

On the outside, my grandfather austere, wavy
hair hanging on black as church shoes past
eighty years old still making babies with bottle
blonde women. *Ugly* my grandmother calls
her husband down the hall, skin jaundiced
yellow. Her sister-in-law's gold tooth capped
with a cut-out heart floating above her sick
bed. *Ugly* like it was his name. *Ugly*, like what
made him ugly? Cadillac man, who are you?
Do you know? And why you travel so far to be
ugly to me? You brought your blonde girlfriend
to your wife's funeral. Ugly. *Ugly* your nickname
for fair and foul reasons, but yours forever,
Ugly. How your mother let you go and raised
the others—ugly. Ugly how the pressure
that sculpted you split you. Ugly the center
of the rock we named you. Ugly the America
that made you then said you was ugly right
up in your face every day, Cadillac man.

The Fruit

I split my tooth on a pleated seed. Skin
as green as watermelon. Disaster
never whispered, just bleeding. An absence
where once the bone held strong. Offensive fruit,
parallel to my childhood. Betrayal
arching over the family I knew least.

I knew my grandfather's Savannah least.
Cool gloved cousins mocked my pimply skin;
the swelling heat, announcing betrayals
that would take years to unfold. Disaster:
the body eating itself. Then this grape—
scuppernong like *scuff-a-nine*. Its absence

in Northern climbs, like a father's absence
proclaiming no relation. Blood, the least
of all ties. My twice great-grandmother's grapes,
her cedar arbor, tart as blood, brown skin,
a sour mother. Family is disaster
written bright across flesh, a betrayal.

Behind every bloodline, a betrayal.
My mother in addiction, in absence,
her run as priestess over disaster.
But she was present in body, at least at least
in mirrors, fretting over her marred skin,
dotting vitamin E, trying for grape

-smooth cheeks. A hopeless wish. A crushed wasp, grapes
scattered as its hive comes. Blood betrayal
unheard of to wasps. Not we beasts with skin.
The doctor tunneled through her, the absence
never left her. I know she loves me least
of her children—the fruit. The disaster.

We dream of blood beneath our nails. Disaster
rhyming with life. A handful of red grapes
swiped from the wasp's mouth. A prayer for the least
protected, who walked off, but were betrayed
by star-spangled covenant. An absence.
A joke. A warranty undone by skin.

Our covenant, disaster. Curse the skin
that leads them to a traitor's feast. Absent
of care for us, wasps know no betrayal.

Peach

The summers swole me: knuckles first, then wrists right down to the elbows.
My family there—richer, unknown to me, and queerly religious. Megachurch
parishioners. Gossips. Voices cantering through the dark with emphatic lilt.
Porch light interrupted only by the salt-sweet of the bread factory and water
bugs churning out steady as if made by the trees. One aunt kind, the other
queer. Religious. House empty of all but lizards and an open bible. Diet
raw. In long skirts and sleeves in heat that swole me. They told me, as all did,
that there was nothing wrong. That I could stand to lose a little weight. Put
me on a diet. Set me to walking around The Oglethorpe Mall in a bright sweatsuit.
Took me to church for the queerness. Left me to wait out a funeral. Invited
me to no funerals, despite how commonly I stayed. Took me out to Vidalia,
teased onions sweet as apples. Sat me at the buffet, but scolded every option.

Slim and swollen as I packed to leave, we explored a tiny tea house. My bracelets
cut into my forearms. A peach baked in filo, honeyed, filled with strawberries.
A pleasure syrupped over months of restriction. An elegance. A half-apology.

Bones

What I learned that summer in Savannah would take years to bloom.
Bracelets too tight on my arm to jingle. A hump at the wrist, cracking
its hopeless melody. The dashing warblers and yellowthroats quarreling
in robes of spanish moss. My grandfather insisted from the car's wheel
that he knew of people who stuffed their mattresses with tufts of green
gray webs. The relationship between the spanish moss and crepe myrtle
is harmony, unison. An extension of the body made perfect by company.
I want to say I saw magnolias but there were only dogwoods' rollicking
pink saucers. All manner of nightly things dropped into them, and rose
reborn in the turgid, listless morning. The body is so dependent. One
fluid displaced by another, barely traceable, and the whole animal folds.
We are not hearty. We are in harmony. We are a unison. Not just bone,
but marrow and fat and lymph coursing in a cycle so fragile it's halted
by a whim. You'd know this if your body was poison to your body. If
at fourteen your body was a slim, smooth-barked tree lashed by an ax.
The tree weeps sap, but it stands—slumped, yes, but alert and lively. In
August, I returned home to New Jersey, was greeted by an oak woods
that smelled like my body because it birthed me. Its shadow enveloped
my shadow. My body had slendered to elbows, to kneecaps, to bones.

Bildungsroman

A poem as a synch of pitching rooms
smearing memory like a wet brush
through watercolor—bright then fade to white
gesso and the arched gesture of painting

faint like children's feet shuffling through the snow
to Taco Bell by the Payless. Barely
one year left of childhood—men say we're grown.
We sing rap parodies to your turtle.

We steal thumb hole shirts from the white girl mall.
We wonder if we'll grow up or if time
will simply stop. Our haunts have not matured,
the swivel stools still sway. Watercolor

strokes festoon the beams that garland registers
and counters in our lean queendom; a place
away from all our homes entail. Quiet
now in the approach of a storm, we feast

to foil, to glitter up lonesome guts
that seem, to us, our sole inheritance.
We Baja Blast with bent down lips. Twilight
hardens the snow to a glimmering threat.

Your father salts the I-95 at night,
while my mother's boyfriend makes copper pipes,
my mother works at the brand new Target.
We think of these as premade lives removed

from glam or grandeur. We want to make poems
of ourselves; we want lush garlands replete
with azalea infernos, peaceful homes.
We want to govern the pitch of our rooms.

Miss Black New Jersey

My grandmother's leopard coat secreted
another leopard coat. Not a lining,
a warning. A real jersey girl sliding
down to her end of her plum pew. Who fitted

white bobby pins over her church nurse hat
into thin silver hair. Imagine her:
a black jersey girl like a persian cat,
glamorous even missing tufts of fur.

Her gloves held their bleach, regardless of grime
until her Avon'd hands flashed into view
as her steering wheel saw fit to remind
her to don leather driving gloves. Her true

love, lifted from the roadside—his five-toed
poodle paws, his unshorn apricot coat.
Yet her sagging towers crushed his throat,
stacks of her cardboard crate collections snowed

their dust across the footworn shag carpet.
He died, but sent to her his best regards
since both knew a township is a tar pit
that traps you in a prefab house of cards.

The pit's a trap, but so too it preserves
her gore-smeared Easter plays, her license plate
with implications too obscene for words,
and the way family spoke about her weight

so aligned with the culture that killed her.
One week, doctor says to smile at the scale.
The next, it's a blockage. The next, she's pale.
One more, she returns to the ground. *Nearer*

My God to Thee then the cemetery.
So here I freeze her in her QVC
plus-size fashions that made her seem to me
New Jersey's one true queen—legendary.

The Sixth International

As the blustering sheets take the shape of bled dark
shadowy forgers shake sleep encased in lead dark.

When the nectar runs thick foragers lick down the neck.
From the tongue a new heat, curves silhouetted dark.

Now the lover won't weep when he leaves to spark streets.
She sleeps as he wished he could sleep—in naked dark.

Whose work is lauded? Whose labor bids no remark
but gliders and sparkers, sleepless, piloted dark?

Each night squinting out the window: sallow torrent
of bright. Moth covens dance, entranced in winnowed dark.

Once, proboscis pried open the tuberose cave
and, passionate, suckled before blushing blood-dark.

Without warning, like sky flame, the door hinge a blade
—the love enters wordless, makes the lover dread dark.

Wind of owls hunting squeeze stamen to piston.
Talons rhyme. Prey threatened, struck wild, then the red dark.

What do moths do, spent from their night light rendezvous?
Near dry beds they lie dead—Con Ed's limited dark.

doppelgänger with seagulls and open legs

the trumpet for the love work inherent in rolling a blunt   an age of praise songs
to a tight blunt   the attentive tongue, damp and flicking as though searching
         for pleasure. a painful, coy foreplay.   owner of any necessary spin
your coney island sugar string of pure pink wind.   it's perplexing, but I think I want to say
the simple thing.   hoops carved into oiled sand   with calloused toe
       or battered, bandaged hands.   when I gurgled up my terror geiser
           ejaculate & ambergris smeared the project of love.
when you breathe
      stale inside our popular elevators   I feel my newly buoyant chest.

o, mine! o, dear! there is a sand-sucked portal
    to our stop on the train before we board the green   and there's room enough
for butterscotch again   salt on your mouth from the rim of the cup
lips parted again by the sopping bit   it's precious, but I think I want to say the sinful thing.

Earth, Earth

If you love someone, tell them—the planet
is dying. Today, I am alone.
The sun warps my southern windows.

The earth itself is human: horny, sad
singular, of changing nature, spiteful—
so our love for her cannot be perfect.

That was never the promise, for humans
love is never perfect, only trying
again. Perhaps the try itself is perfect.

The feathered thing that does not fly. A gust
back in the attic, never out from it.
Today, I live in Brooklyn, Baltimore

Yesterday: Savannah. Oakland, alone
in Jack London Square clutching pink flowers.
I ponder prices of spinach, too high

for money barely gathered! In pride month!
(Perhaps the fairest price is five bucks, but
the wage it swipes is eternally gone.)

Today, I am in Philadelphia
holding a restraining order, photos
of my bitten limbs and the poems torn

down to their iambs by hands I once chose
to hold me. Now I am buying an eighth
for that burnt down memory. I'm walking

through a flood in thrifted boots, soles a maze
of holes, praying on the good of the earth,
the earth who, if no one else, is perfect.

Riley says *the earth is dying.* That's why
I want children, I insist, *wise black children*
who are close to their mother, the black earth.

Who empathize with her bitten limbs, who
sort out her problems with the fast brilliance
endemic to all black children. In space

they'll hover above, see what's to be done.
Maybe they won't have to go it alone.
Maybe they'll have company in other

people's children. Or aliens. Or rocks.
(I've heard they will cry out under certain
conditions, what could they be waiting for?)

Or Jesus, surely Jesus cared about
the earth, sure, the desert was a tan blur
but those gilt views! I assume, however,

they'll be in space. Peeking from round windows
overhead, they'll gaze down at her: walls, tracks
that stud her wide waist, her vast, saline cheeks

just a face in the dark. Wild green afro
unpicked since the dawn of time. They'll love her
perfectly, save her with archaic words

my elders knew enough to pass to me.
A great chain sent to heal the earth, although
healing her imperfectly, partially.

We straw up oil from each accident,
metabolize the soil meant to kill
our mothers, send poison through our bloodline

waiting for help she shouldn't need, the earth
looking towards us, indifferent but needful.
Tell her you love her. The earth is dying.

I love you and

since I never
read a poem about collards   cooked sour
in a burnt, black pan, here's an ode
to your winter   greens cooked too quick
with too much vinegar, my forever nigga.
I find your greens too hard, but you
still my nigga—a stockpot for you, a bowl
another heaping plate for you, all of it.
Have it all. I love you and your tart greens.
A challenge to the tongue, never the heart.

psychedelia

As quick and quiet as a small yet precious object swallowed by deep water. Whispers everywhere; lips flutter asking their lovers who will survive America? We name those already struck from the list. Each crisis punctuated by a crisis. North Jersey's factories blank as dead faces. Ports with no dockers. An unshakable aura of shortage and lack. The softest erosions ferried us to this shore. Our *we* fragmented, atomized, and blown away.

They slashed the knit of our deft nets: Callen-Lorde; Women Organized Against Rape; Women Against Abuse; Planned Parenthood; Streetwise and Safe; Safe Outside the System; Medicaid; Medicare; Social Security; Disability Services; the VA; CHIP; WIC; SNAP; re-entry programs; ESL; Job Corps; senior centers; school breakfast programs; school lunch programs no grand declaration, but no money either. Even those contested spaces, the snake-led non-profits, evaporated.

Only then the windswept fiats. First the things on which no one could agree; the lifestyle questions that unite traditional Americans. Those death machines; those family breakers. The panic generators. We embraced the hedonism that is our birthright. We hidin our parades, play parties, bars, raves, game nights & in the arms of our lovers. And then the insurance companies merged. We became preexisting conditions. We extended our run as conditional citizens.

Alisha queues three hours at the pharmacy behind mothers, their wailing children, and elders whose legs wobble with effort. The technician snips her insurance card in two, empathetic head nodding. Both brown skin women filmed with sweat, now air conditioning isn't expected, they submit to the premature summer. She bursts from the store, dark eyes pounding. No diabetes medicine. No birth control. She clears her mind for the tasks ahead, her private back-up plan.

Who can survive America? An experiment in sparking wires, poisonous spines outstretched for adornment. An elder ascends, crumpled suit and frosted hair, ready for the great nationalist run. He rumbles tyrannical sound. Cherub lips & thin eyebrows artlessly plucked. He is braggadocio & bravado to the assenting crowd. He chooses America's survivors with microphone & pen: slow gun & sharp cock. Someone cheers, but not here. Someone profits, but not us. The casualties.

Alisha walks three miles home. She barely makes it across the bridge without spilling over its guardrails. She puts her cat up for adoption through the whisper network, drags her furniture to the curb. She calls her mother from a payphone: no answer and wasted change. She greets a nice, white family who wants Bastet. In her pink bathtub, swallowed by foam and blossoms, she swallows stockpiled Ativan with E&J. Everything slowed to a halt, leaving only lavender & bolted door.

I knew Alisha better than the last suicide. Tall femme top of the scene; two years ago we dissolved the quick weave glue and buzzed her a tapered peach, the lumps of skull carved out from ancient braids. She wore long wigs in transit to honey blonde locs. Royal gap femme sailing over a hopefully excellent elsewhere now. Her mama, prayer warrior and homo hater, arrives from elsewhere on a tidal wave of *Why? How?* to collect her. *Who's responsible?* Who indeed.

Every death drags reality clattering into our rooms. Parents long disowned, lovers who abandoned, provoking the madness that triggered the headlong spiral, cops with their point-toothed smirks and searchlights. Partners left without enough money for rent; honored thieves feast on absences they created, profit from our disasters. The mother wonders aloud *who did this to my baby?* The child she gathered for suck, who grew into the pervert she spurned.

Did the rough fact of her rejection appear to her as she arrived, or would she have to wait and see the body laid out on two wooden tables pushed together, fresh from a freezer of our own design? Would she need to hear the bell on the coroner's truck? Would she need to hear the silence of the ambulance, watch us wait, watch us realize it would never come? Who could tell by her face, rigid with shock, as we made way for her to make her way? Who could know if she knew what she made.

Whatever she thought of the life that her daughter'd been living, whatever she thought of us, all so much like the child she'd abandoned, our tattooed wingspans, our easy laughter, the shine of our internal silver wells turned loose, she fell into the chair we left for her—just beyond the bullhorn that served as our microphone—and reached for the nearest hand, which reached back, and others followed extending tissues and flowers, cocktails and cards and near worthless dollar bills.

The assembled parties stood, feet stuck to the floor clinging hard to unmopped liquor, while the loved ones take turns sobbing sanitized anecdotes into the microphone. Perched on a high stool at the bar, I heard a few through the fritz of dying batteries and her mother's wails. Asar scrubbed glasses, swept behind the counter. His shift started in four hours. He had opened the bar as a favor to her partners and as final reverence to the blessed dead.

Beautiful Falsettos, the last of our places. Gay by percentage. We had the bar midweek and Saturday, Pride weekend, Thanksgiving, and Christmas. Otherwise, we mixed with neighborhood regulars who commandeered the jukebox, old heads who knew we ain't know nothin' about this or that, lonely stragglers of every persuasion, and a ragtag, insurgent drag show like a masquerade ball where you could meet anyone even another part of your own self. And Asar behind the bar.

Who did this to my baby girl? She asks at the emergency meeting in smoky Falsettos, packed so tight the security folks sit on splintered window ledges. Asar fixes her a strong drink, on the house. She settles down. *Why didn't someone call me? I could've come got my baby. We woulda took a collection; I'd've found a way.* Black as we are, we've learned to respect the flimsy shell of grief. Men pass her cigarettes and cocktails until she's ready to see the body at the funeral home a block away.

All forty or so guests present exit the bar to find daylight. I wonder aloud to Asar about how the mother would pay for a funeral:

ASAR
Didn't she already say she'd have to take up a collection at her church? The funeral is for her anyway. I'm sure she'll figure it out.

To pay a church and a graveyard now seems a waste of time and money—it lives in the privileged space beyond work or barter.

Alisha's note asked that her mother take down her altar. Everything else she owned redistributed to replace the things we could not otherwise afford. Once, we took an ecclesiastic acid trip, all our visions infused with church hurt. I imagine her body paraded through the aisles of a house that rotted her self-understanding, that insisted she cross her legs at the ankles, and that taught her to sing. *I bet you ten dollars the preacher she hated most does her service. I hope she haunts everybody.*

ASAR

First of all, we both know you ain't got ten dollars unless you "borrowed" ten dollars from me—

Actually, I borrowed $20, but I didn't mention it. *I'll pay him back before he notices,* I reassure myself.

ASAR

—and second, Alisha don't care. She dead. The funeral is for the living. All they're gunna do is sing over the body, lie about her, and put her dead ass in the ground.

I read agitation in his body: *so you wouldn't care if you died and they gave you a funeral in a church? You lyin'.*

He stopped for a moment, the sides of his head shaved to hide the smooth patches, and gathered his body up straight, both feet flat to the grimy sidewalk, hand clutching the crook of his wooden cane, and sucked his teeth.

ASAR

What do you mean? I was an usher!

To me, this was a cope, a cop out. *I just don't see how it would make any difference if I'm dead*, he insisted. But he was closer than I to whatever comes after, so I let the conversation hover between us.

I reach for his hand. He shrugs away to avoid it. I forget myself, I don't remember what I thought I was doing. In silence, we continue. In silence we arrive back to my—our—apartment. Wouldn't do to bring it up, too dangerous to fight and lose his scent hanging in the doorway when he says he'll be right back. Too dangerous. Without his burned hands, arm tattoo descending just beneath the wrist? Wouldn't do without the comfort of another body radiating its desires. Understand, it wouldn't do.

THIS PAGE LEFT INTENTIONALLY BLANK

I repack my bag for an overdue visit to an absent friend. I prepare with both kinds of excitement. A book, since he is certain to be late. Two decks of playing cards: one for his two player version of spades, the other for reading. A photo of us years ago at the conference pulled from the pocket of an old suitcase. We are young and unsmiling, our clothes a key to the styles that dressed the earliest parts of this century: nameplate belts, shield sunglasses, spaghetti straps, and a tall tee.

I meet Shalimar in the park over the water now packed with the dead and the living. I sip a bottle of hooch from my shorts. He seems untethered. I ask how he's doing. He avoids the question, but the lag in his speech and repetition alarms me. It's my business and none of my business, and what can I do about it anyway. The visit isn't unpleasant. It's always a comfort to be around him. His stern jaw is clenched, his skin tight over each inch of him. And, I think, I smell iron.

I start my calculations: his tattoos are bumpy with scars but not wounds; his dingy white tee shirt unbloody, if soiled—he didn't wince when I hugged him; the domed front of his jeans are harder to scope, but nothing out of the ordinary. The inseams—

SHALIMAR

Whatchu starin' at so hard, man? I thought you were past all that!
You tryna catch a peek!

He caught me so I had to tell him. *I smell blood. Are you bleeding?* His face deflates; my math becomes his. He licks his chipped front tooth out of habit but says nothing.

Neither of us mentions what process has started. He enters the putrid brick bathroom. I wait outside. *You good?* I offer as he emerges, face blank like those who have seen a spectral visage. His quiet is enough to know the answer. *Come home with me,* I beg him. *Come home with me and we'll figure something out.* Knowing there will be tension if not fighting. Full aware of the most likely outcome of this extended kindness. How could I leave him without leaving him to die?

We walk close together through the turnstile, the end of all my funds. We make it to the other side. We know we'll have to walk. We stop amidst the crowd of lovers on the bridge, some untouched by these tragedies, others spooning on concrete.

SHALIMAR

Whatever you think this is doing is not what it's going to do.
I was fine staying out there. I can take care of myself.

I ignore him. I've known him long enough to anticipate the spiral that awaits us. We'll all figure it out when we get home.

Two hours of walking later, I sink my key into the knob and swing open our splintering door. *Don't sit on my couch though,* I advise before we get inside. We're perpetually low on medical supplies around here, so I hand him a set of clean, black crew socks and he slips into the bathroom. *Dr. Bronner's in the cabinet over the toilet* I yell through the door. I find some clothes to fit him on Asar's side of the closet. I tack a sign on the entrance: SHALIMAR INSIDE, FIX YO' FACE.

We take shots off the lil home brew that I made—liquid burn to help open the conversation. Why hold on to it instead of investing in pleasure. *I lost my job*, I say as though he was cognizant, *six months ago*. He inverts the bottle above open lips, arms begging gravity for just a little more liquor, just a little more drunk. *Did you hear me*, I wonder aloud to him as he thumps the bottle's glass onto the counter. He doesn't answer, so I continue: *I don't know how I'll find work.*

THIS PAGE LEFT INTENTIONALLY BLANK

And still, there's always work. I raise plants in a block of open space—Chiron's Green. It used to be a row of homes, black folks owned every one. Until Chiron Jackson was executed. His blood stained his own stone steps as he added to the garbage heap that spanned from curb to curb. They didn't even bother trying to claim a crime. They just wanted his house to crack open his block and impose their version of peace. They just said they couldn't have known he was safe, so they shot.

Before all that, Chiron founded Red, Blaq & Greens Urban Farm. He taught kids how to grow food. Employed folks coming home from prison and war. He hosted neighborhood meetings and pride month events. Organizers agreed to do teach-ins in exchange. We enjoyed even our grouchiest neighbors. We worried less. We were still soft enough to be surprised by what came next. His homestead burned hours after his death. His neighbors pushed out into uncertainty.

He was my neighbor, my only straight friend and, at times, my employer. He knew Asar ever since since, when he and Asar's mama used to go together. An organic intellectual. One day I caught him popping his fingers to Janelle Monáe while he read *The Black Athena* laid out on his miniscule front lawn. We delivered netted black plastic crates to food pantries full of spinach carrots tomatoes strawberries blueberries summer corn and we made plans to expand. We all ate good, and extra.

He wasn't the first one they took, but he was the first everyone noticed. Chiron was a presence, we each felt his excisement from our street and our lives. Little children wandered by the rotting farm, plucked root vegetables from dry dirt by their green heads, ate berries from twisted vines, but couldn't register what changed. We were like those children: alarmed & sad. We gathered, three and four at a time, in the open mouths of door frames, repeating the story from other angles.

There was no time to think before the next one was cut down. The progeny of each tragedy were many, a cycle of open palms in the sky then bullets, bayonets then tears and shouting and the gurgling street on foot and the drum/chant/cry then open palms then bullets then tears then shouting then street then drum chant cry palms bullets tears shout street drum chant cry palms bullets (bayonets) tears shout street drum chant cry palmbullettearshoutstreetdrumchantcrypalmbulletbulletbullet

Things quieted later, yes, but on that first night, we raged. Everyone who heard the shots waited a moment, then emerged from their apartments to bear witness. No one called. No one planned. We knew Chiron. We loved Chiron. Now his blood flooded his just-swept stoop. Perhaps, shock dominated: not knowing what to do, we did without knowing, the way arms push up from the ground after a blow to the head. The way men shot as they run (just for a moment) continue.

The response was rapid, it was everyone in the street all at once. Factions, rivalries, feuds—they didn't come until after each night felt like a disappointing block party, like fucking all night but nobody cums. It was satisfying until we realized we were nobody. We demanded power, the cops shot into the crowds. We dwindled to a regime of the childless, of men without families, those refused work at every job, season after season, queer, trans, who lost everything or had nothing worth losing.

Those who returned to the edges of the neighborhood found their apartments occupied by patrolmen. They wandered into the street, dazed by unanticipated destitution, never given the time to collect a change of clothes before their exile. Bashfully, they turned up on the doorsteps of whomever's address they recalled. We flung open our wide doors, donated our extra bedrooms and now-useless home offices, until we too were permitted only to the edge of the neighborhood, or to an exit.

THIS PAGE LEFT INTENTIONALLY BLANK

Shalimar fell asleep in his blanket fort. Asar opens the door, moving slowly, his hand swollen over his cane. I tell him he has a fever, as though he doesn't already know. *What the fuck is going on?* flashes in my brain. *What the fuck is going on?* He sighs, *did you hear about Troy?* Another name in a list of names, tethered to ropes and stretched between two identical horses: one that pulls us through the year, the other desperately bucking in nostalgia's direction. They are often equally yoked.

Whisper networks activated: a cacophony of silent alarms. Contagious is what we call it, grab our lovers by their quaking wrists, smooth down our best friend's eyebrows with our thumbs and breathe the spores of them that meet the air in and in and in. Mema said death comes in threes. Ostensibly, she was straight. Death comes over for coffee here. Death shows up to work three hours late. Death peers from behind your new fuchsia curtains, wears the fleece slippers you gifted.

Death arrives first for those you left behind: the homie you forgot to call who you knew took rejection personal; the sick queers, soon-to-be-dead queers; the drama queen you hated but admired for her rudeness, though not the identities with which she'd attempt to obscure it, who'd always announce in the fight *this is why I'm going to kill myself* until one day, she did; go ahead, feign surprise, you never saw this coming. It came: through the lips, around the throat, hitting its mark—inside.

A chosen death, its accessibility makes it feel nearly mandatory. No healthcare but euthanasia. Wild stigma relieved only in life undone, an absence that seems inevitable. When a body's borders were constructed poorly, or porously. When the body you built appears in no books, no movies, not even reality TV. You're gone before you ever started. You're a joke even to your lovers. You came from nowhere and were formed by no mold. When the body you claim is named otherwise everywhere else.

Shalimar and I started T at the same time. We're brothers in the weird, fraternal world of trans guy friendship. He likes to pretend we didn't fuck, for several years & not at all sporadically, but that's sort of what's required. If real men not gay then you have to be straight to be a man. That's all he ever wanted, all he ever was. When I say it out loud to you that sounds so sad to me. Only things that make perfect sense can be as tragic. Shalimar lives in the world, subject to actual reality.

So you try your best to keep it together, to become legible, to make sense as best you can. In this sense, I envy both the men before me. I acknowledge their attempt as far more sincere than my own. I know as well as anyone the peculiar rigor of their self-denial. The charming affect stomped out to pass during phone calls. The scraps of their past they most miss. For a while, the confines of our lives had dulled the specter of our prior reality, but we found the inner coal of hate, and lit it.

This is why a room with more than one straight man becomes a small room. The air grows thick with their musk as they indulge their permanent desire to stretch out. Whether brother, friend, or lover, they are all a beautiful burden wrapped up in your generous love. These two are my always men. Their straightness is no barrier to their love, but stewards all their actions. Every turn a time to wonder how much it costs me to love them privately, or what part in me they gratify.

Shalimar wakes up as I silence my shot day alarm. I crawl past the droopy blanket flaps into his cave and sit next to his feet. His eyes are open staring at nothing. I poke his soles, which tap back at my fingernail. Now here comes the puke. Internally I commend myself for putting down bleach-stained towels. *I can't live like this*, he tells me as though I don't know, as if anyone could. We live a life with no margin of error and an open vein as a safety net.

When he says *I can't*, I know he means *I won't*. He starts to cry, surprised to have regained the ability. It's one of the first things to go—before the first thread of beard, or your voice deepens. Then you're losing someone or overwhelmed or having a shitty day and your eyes are dry and something feels stuck in you. Emotional constipation. He covers his face with both arms. I ask if he wants to split the end of my vial, a fraternal courtesy. You don't eat in front of company, you offer a plate.

So far as I can tell, there's about 2.5 mgs, which is two full doses for me, but I only have one syringe left and two needles since the swap ran out of literally everything. I wet some bunched up toilet paper with 90% ABV and swiped it over the nipple. (Alcohol swabs were the first pleasantry to go.) White curds speckle the bottle and collect where its metal rim meets rubber. I bought it so I take first shot; more blood than I anticipated waves back. I use the same clump to blot the flow.

Shalimar's injection technique is trepidatious to the point where I'm like *just hurry up and inject it, Jesus, shoot it into your goddamn muscle and be done with it, like how can you be so macho yet so unable to perform this basic function of your life?* He extends it and asks *can you do it?* It's cloyingly intimate, but I say, *fine, it's easier in your butt.* He's huffy but agrees it's the most comfortable spot to inject another. His asscheeks are ashy but what could I expect from a straight boy? Shea butter.

Ok, so it's uncharitable to crack on his mangy appearance knowing what caused it. I am aware. I am delicate. He's wearing Asar's clothes and his face is shut tight as a stitched wound until I let him know it's finished.

ASAR
*Y'all done with whatever thing you got goin'
on in the bathroom? I'm not askin' no questions
but I gotta get ready for work.*

And I'm like pause. because he's actually too sick to go to work. I let Shalimar get decent, even though he mumbled some shit about *these gay niggas* under his breath, mostly as a reflex.

THIS PAGE LEFT INTENTIONALLY BLANK

In the morning, conversations zip through the streets, leaping long parked cars to enter welcoming doors. I bike to the farm to start my work. My orange backpack rattles its clasp. Nettles, burdock, and plantago from the tarry soil beside the disused road. Ramp from the edge of a drying river's bed. Hush-hush roses from a forbidden bush. The yield of two pots of wild violets. A garden box that motherwort devoted to itself. Prolific mint that leaps any obstacle. All the dandelions you can eat.

Each stop a warm light, we pull the one hitter, they pay as able. Or not. A service, not a business. I am the first that it helped, so I share what I have learned with the generosity of my teachers. We spread around what we have, more so now, crushed between the palms of a great dying. I've been fortunate. The disappeared are not mine and I am thankful, so I shuttle Jolette, Alisha's girlfriend, a satchel of motherwort and violet tea. One breaks; we break. Heal one; heal we.

Jolette cracks the door to address my knock, her features unfamiliar & elongated by bereavement. Her face makes me question why I came. Did I interrupt her fragile ritual? Were there instructions I couldn't possibly know? She is slick with tears. She flips her hand towards the chair, and invites me to sit in her new reality. The tea, in its paper bag, on the table. Though her water first runs brown, she waits for it to run clear, then makes a flame below the tarnished kettle.

I hadn't expected her to talk much; my visits are surprises. A few still have phones of their own, land lines that splice words into primal sound. The listeners left with expensive vocal snow and proof of love, but no message. Good thing everyone's home now. The upside of the downside. Without jobs, we raise chickens on rooftops; cook abundantly; we repair, forage, plant, and solder; we make love, hold each other accountable; ask *how you doin'* and actually listen to the answer.

Once communication became luxury we started to build genuine community. Healer home visits. Crisis meetings at Falsettos. Vast houses warmed by cardboard box heaters. According to Jolette, the dreamy mechanic who lives below rigged some solar panels from CDs. *How she keeps fuel in that motorcycle is the real question.* Jolette chokes a phlegm-coated laugh: *beats me*, she admits, *maybe she has secret money. A lot of them do.* Her spindly fingers bent around her shallow mug.

Motherwort: won't she do it? Bright grin of broad leaves open in their cluster. Tender purple flowers like slight, high bells adorning slender stalks. Mumming the sleeplessness and gut hurt that the dead leave. The hunger it carries stops wasting, flesh chewing its own flesh. Help us find the cooling heart, lay hands, rub. Improves the body's blood movement and pushes through collapsing corridors. Hums and plucks and perks up the flattened parts. Returns us to our estranged bodies.

I come home to the same warm home. Calamari's lint blossom tail bobbing near the door, hungry and screaming. Shalimar's slippers under the table, his wide, flat feet planted above. The chair belongs to Calamari, her gray fur muddling its tweed. Endless wooden shelving my man built from detritus. Enough space and place for all the life that stays with us. Goldfish bowls and aquariums from which vines sprout. Leaves sag over their metal lips, unabashedly flopped. A life. A home.

In the luminous afternoon, Asar's sputter has become a cough. Just a slight one. His lupus meds down to the last half-moon, the amber bottles long dwindled. There's no way of telling how much it'll cost this time. *Put it out of your mind.* We'll find a way. The farm pays fine for now and if it doesn't, I'll trade something better. I don't care, I'll steal it. Find another way. Here comes the spiral. The fear engine. Disaster anticipator. Semi-logical waves ripple out from the heart of my mind.

I compel him to bed. I heat water in the copper kettle, settle into night clothes and soft voices. I untangle his hair, his nose pressed into my side. The cat wants in; I have enough hands. He is petulant with sleep hunger:

ASAR

> *Maybe I'll sleep behind the bar tonight.*
> *Maybe I'll sleep on the floor.*

Sleep wherever you want, go wherever it is you've been going, but you've been testy since the funeral. Let it go.

He falls into the sheets, my hand against the thin skin of his chest. I feel him straining to breathe. *It's no problem*, I assure myself, but I'm uncertain. I'll check in the morning.

Then to Shalimar, his eyes trained on the ceiling, impossibly still. Who was not saved from funk by a hot shower. Who has filled the living room with the aroma of traps and snares that grow larger with the clock's lines. Who tells me he won't be staying long, that he thinks he'll head back tomorrow. What will he do, I ask knowing it's only partly my business, feeling it's the most pressing business I have. He rolls to face me. *I'll do what I was doing*, he tells me before closing his eyes.

Oh Shalimar, whom I once loved, what if those weren't the last breaths we breathed in each other's quarters? What if a bright red life was open and free among us, warming our guts, inviting spaciousness? What if there was a flight you could catch to spirit yourself to yourself? Would you have stayed on the ride? What would it take for us to still have you, know you? Who was it you always thought you would become? How would he have advised you in those warped hours before?

We cannot know what happened as you slipped from our door into the indigo evening, almost as blue as the hue hung from your shoulders—a mute aura, you man gone too soon to bloom. We cannot know the mercenary, but the cost still ours to bear—a little bit of money searched for in our sleep, enough to break whatever was left of me when we found you slumped and gone, face pressed into the stoop's iron rail. Ours to bear, and bear alone. You, who never bloomed, are gone.

THIS PAGE LEFT INTENTIONALLY BLANK

Last year: discarded iron becoming old blood in the long rain. We found a hardness that insisted we continue, a carnivorous hardness subsisting on a diet of let blood. A gate around my heart alone since no one knew you or no one knew you like I knew you. Now there's no one to know. The calendar assaults me; I am a victim of time spent without you. Days overgrown as the space you carved in me, the parts of me that hollowed to fit you still retain their shape, ever they remain the same.

A toe for your ankles rimmed by stolen sneakers; the others for your halo as a Yankees fitted so long ago we were barely more than children; the Nascar jacket that sweat glued against your deep brown back. An ear for the sneak of a smile when you'd cheat at Uno. A tooth for every straight tooth, and for the gap that split them into two evenly matched armies. My liver for how you shone when you loved yourself enough for grease; a kidney for you in your white shirt, starched & bleached.

The pocket money you spent to overdose seemed as it should to only be a splinter in a larger account, but that well was drying and the grieving cost more than I first assumed. Spoiled labor days, nights exhaled over bottles hauled to the detritus congested curb come noon. It was too much. It was too soon. Apartments around us warmed with the shouts of couples moving couches down the stairs, into the street, for trucks headed elsewhere—if they were lucky, if the job held, if—

Or else. Or else the couch moved by only two in silence, into the street, at the gutter joining the choir of ruin. A banner year for rats. A decent year for feral cats long tossed across the threshold, their names and statuses changed in an instant. A year feared by pigeons, put to work if not eaten, or put to work before being consumed. A year for the crows who surveyed the sidewalk in search of a feast. A year for nails hung with grim formalities. A year for cops. A year for preachers and pimps.

A year for bodies carried to the curb to wait for a coroner's truck to roll through after the end of ambulances. A year later the streets strewn with high pyres and the animal ritual of grief. A year of scavenging the city's skeleton for splintering wood, finding only steel and yellow newspapers, and our palms torn in two painlessly until nightfall. A year of concomitant hells bearable only when viewed at a squint. A year of endless debate about where to go next, or if there even was a next place to go.

A year with few options for escape—strikes on the train, sanctions on the failing banks. A black mark spread across every ceiling as the holes in the roof grew and opened up, light coursing through their makeshift skylights. Even the landlords sought other places, other schemes. They moved into their buildings with no hope of paying up without another's pockets. They couldn't afford another fifty dollar eviction. They knew they could not escape with their lives.

Before spring we planted, sure we would reap through May. That worked before the price of water shriveled the gardens. By June, there was nothing but a wither of potatoes, forgotten in last winter's dirt. There was no escape, just the distraction of an empty mind. We paid dearly for berries. We foraged for green. But we saw what was next, our exit clear and bold as a birth. We sought comfort, in a blunt, in a man, in a tab that brought color back to the world.

A torn edge worth its price for the ability to bend light through life. As the money dwindled, and everything we owned cardboard-crated, or shuffled from our home to exist among refuse, there was yet that hope. That square. Those waking dreams that made reality bearable. On the squalid stoop where I finally found you. By the ruins of places I've loved, at their edge, sea spray prevailing over whatever still exists. Living on fumes from shimmering visions. Plodding home in the snow.

And now, on the day of departure, among the leftover dust peopling the hardwood floor, waterlogged rug long abandoned by the roadside, and still waiting as we pass along the sidewalk. My old roommate escaped to Michigan, to his silver origins. His ilk leap towards tenure or massage school or tattoo school. Me and all I know well are rocketing into the green unknown. To unfamiliar towns in an attempt to people them, to start again in a place we didn't choose. Cheaper rent, but not home.

But first to start the probably dead cars or to find neighbors with a charge to jump you. First to evict the vermin building homes within the seats, or to cover the punctured leather seats, or rub the algae from the windshield, to dig two fingers into an exhaust pipe and pull out dead leaves, to reckon the spider's nest your glove box has become, to take a test drive around three silent blocks to see if travel is possible, let alone feasible. First to indulge your vanity with a car cleaned by dirty water.

The rejected on either side of the road, cast away city, no harvest for the removed. The ones who slept lean familiar in doorways, stoops, on corners. They are spreading out on lawns, making homes of parks where they were once swept away in the night for no discernable reason. Swooped from on high by a powerful scope. Did we shield them? Did we now leave them to die in the next rain? We did our best, we whisper into other fretful ears, midnight behind us—a polite, encouraging lie.

City of iron buried in alloy, sold in parts for scrap. August sweat. Every avenue sopped with bodies down the coast, only a trickle away from us, as it's been for months of weekend. For a moment, same song on all radios lifts a hum above our foreheads. For a moment people dancing at a red light. For a moment, a moment more at home, whatever's left, whatever can be spared. The horns threaten soon as the green light winks, as amusement devolves into door slams and expletives.

The floods. Their living ghosts. The smell of the fungi reclaiming damp cardboard and moss and shadowy mold, digesting the bathrooms and kitchens of our vacant apartments. The water-loving things returning, or themselves migrating lower on the continent—mosquitos, diseases, lice, deaths and those rising to greet it—snakes, gators, pests, pollinators all engaged in the great, new movement of the day each searching for a home that will not sink, however unlikely.

My mother's grave underwater somewhere in this abandoning city. I leave to mourn somewhere more permanent. Highways full of other mourners agree we are but a single body shuttling loss through its veins. We are cells to one another. We knew ones lost in their affordable basements. We knew ones gasping at the dimmed light on their machine, an external organ blinkered by the power outages. We remember the ones waiting for the eye of the pharmacy to flick awake, the pills never came.

Me? Well, I never had time to consider that gauze stuffed our foundation where steel was rumored to be. Never thought about what would happen if the wheels that shuttled oranges, or lightbulbs, or lettuce, or dress shirts, whether seamed with fragile whirls of string or before the assembly, lumps of cotton husks on a ship, on a truck in a basket, or yes, the pills, or the medicinal oils, or the sharps that inject it, or the plastics which house it for travel, that life could (simply, quietly) stop.

For it had never stopped for me. Always some job. Alway some distraction from myself. Some feigned sense that what existed did so in perpetuity, a portrait of my naivety cast before me as a shadow. I took *settled* for *set*, never imagined a shake in the heart of the beast below the pavement, the hungry king, mouth nothing but a money funnel shoveling what he can from every pocket, shoveling what escapes from about our feet into the sewers, where the gators wait. Where we dare not follow.

The money having fled from our purses, the city abandoned us to trees and diminutive houses in a nameless place, unknown and unmapped in our hubris. We knew we'd change their names to city; no reason to become too familiar. We'd yank out its unblemished teeth. We'd build a culture that mirrors what we lost and sit at the edge of our new claim sighing toward the breathing wreckage and swear we saw it wink back at us, flirting and licking its lips. We practiced the language of mirage.

We shrunk as we unlatched from the city's spent breast, drained of all but her heaving wire frame. The car full to choking and topped by a mattress; two cats—one sweet, one imperious, or perhaps a lone cat, two-minded and temperamental; thirty some-odd pairs of shoes, all but three belonging to the man who clenched the steering wheel, distressed as the city shrunk behind us, pounding the blank radio, cursing inaudibly at other drivers.

Asar's cigarette bent out of the driver's window—a little lantern in the chaos, illuminating a bright spot in his safety mirror. To watch him do anything is pleasure, even to watch him suffer. It isn't love, is nothing, is a mirror, a friendship, a courtship, a bed, an open secret made perhaps too obvious, like getting caught doing something you swore you wouldn't, struggling beneath your own lie, suffering inside your delusion when everyone had made their peace.

I ruminate about our small closet worth of wardrobe, my boxes containing too few socks and too many black briefs, my typewriter with nearly untouched keys, a fraction of cherished books, his family pictures, his pull-up bar, and twenty-four packets creamy ramen noodles, stalling down the halted road. Miles of gas lines we thought were traffic. Our little caravan, fretting behind us, beaming a loop with us, taking different exits, subject to fate's stammering clock, fair only in inconveniences.

The other cars still sparser even than ours, sometimes containing just the bodies, half-clothed and dirty. He checks behind us to find his mother's upraised arm: everything managed. His brothers play fight on the cloth back seats. We'll figure it out when we get there, we can figure it out. On either side of the highway: people squatting uncovered and urgent, falling out, laying prostrate, others hovering over, muttering vague prayers—a pattern. Then, finally, we got there.

When we arrive, at the good enough house of too-few rooms, always too few rooms, we find there is a fence, a gate some would say, in the back, bearing a stamp of blank red earth in its ramshackle embrace. And, just like a man, he turns to me and says, pointing: I'll put my weight bench over there. What weight bench? What shipment? What money? A delicious hopeful nothing to bless the endless travel, to punctuate the end of something beloved, to memorialize his resisted exile.

He unpacks the cars with his brothers, a study in lankiness, its odd efficacy and uncanny strength. They drop the mattress. They add no sheets. I drag the sheets around the corners, tuck them against the linoleum floor. Pry open the window with a butter knife, watching the painted ledge go white to brown like a sucked jawbreaker. I blow my cigarette into the open air, reach for one unmown dandelion, pluck it and inspect the hollow tube of its stem at the break. It bleeds.

I move it to a plastic tumbler, water turning red around it. A feeling like the frost approaching. A slip of the tongue or of the soil. A mistake. Perhaps the dirt? Perhaps the harvest? Perhaps the region? Perhaps my mind, lost in the forgettings of the day. Maybe it had always been as it is and I instead am new. I find the bag where I smuggled my last tab. I return my head to the portal, hoping to remain hidden. What? Out the window? *Shalimar? Shalimar. Shalimar!*

Shalimar with no shoes on the sidewalk. Shalimar who could have been our neighbor. Shalimar, who I remembered as a duty I failed to fulfill. Shalimar nodding off on the Path train. Shalimar bleeding in the park. Shalimar, more potential than good works. Now he's a figure clothed in the fantasy of another beginning, before his contours are enveloped once more by the here after here. I crane my neck to confirm his form. Asar slips into our sheets with dirty feet. A lock clicks.

Instantly, he sleeps beside me. I roll uneasy through a weak rest, fractured dreams half-recalled. From the window, a green stirring, a singing on the breeze. The woods itself a life, an entity, demanding care or love or attention. Everything that can be done is done for attention, the sole economy of the universe. The green approaches. A spilled soft saucer becomes a green wool beanie. Then, from crown to feet, here comes Shalimar, silent as ever, solemn, gesturing to the waiting trees.

There must be a place where something grows. The trees collaged around our dirt like verdant, hovering clouds, kinky and urgent, begging, chanting me over, and since I have nowhere to be I am free to heed them. Soon I am washed in a wheel of ancient starlight, its blank screen dragged on twilight's cracked left heel. Their close talk enters me, shines into me and out of my shocked mouth, a simple beam of old light made perfect by its retelling, from lip to lip across time.

In my backward sight, a portrait of trees, the organic tangle of black walnut skin, gold leaves tickertaped across the highway. Our tires whining, unenlightened, mourning our progress — few truly regard the descent of quotidian objects. Only held in mortal esteem when shattered or misplaced, and even then, only barely, as if interchangeability should foreclose upon gratitude even in this country of the object as god, of money as religion, of political banks, of lucrative holy wars.

My guide on this journey a flake, a half-starter. The surprising
reveal of who truly has personal power, with a rich anointing,
an odd inheritance fulfilled through walking before
me—spectral yet imposing. Dogged whilst serving the needs of
the bloodline and its whims. This man who, when alive, never
mentioned god, who seemed to evade all spiritual identity.
Now, an authority, now responsible, the righteous one among
us standing in for the rich and mysterious godhead.

I tell him as I explain to you but he then pointed through me:

SHALIMAR
O, you so accustomed to liminality, to escape, to longing, to the
unrequited, the prayers you stuffed into the inbox of a lazy god.
You are unacquainted with liberation. Here it's best to leave a
little slip. Watch me do it, and you'll learn the steps.

Next his arms angled and feathered, the feet sharpened to three
spiked points, his nose and mouth beaked together, and I grow
shy having never really known him and believing I had.

Then he becomes a pigeon at my feet wearing a Yankee fitted, a puffer jacket, and timbs. A negro harpy. A scholar and a terror like the others—freed from what preceded him, preceded us. Then, to easy flight like part of the breeze, just showing off. And from his wing falls a stained napkin that reads: *you must walk through two cities, and the four additional blocks. When you reach the black-owned dry cleaners, evade or engage the double-dutch assassins.*

SHALIMAR

Be confronted by the unfact of your once girlhood: its bo-bos, its
plastic poodle barrettes and the ones that look like bows, its
excruciating white tights, its white patent leather shoes and
undeniable danger—

—I mean, well, anyway, fill your apron with lavender gumballs and bring them back home. I have no apron. From his filthy wing falls a white bolt of felt, which I tie into knots at my waist and the nape of my neck.

SHALIMAR

Rub it for advice. Swath your head with it for protection. Drape
it around your shoulders if you get cold. It never misses. And
don't look for me. I'll be back when you've done all you can.

O dear felt bolt: Damn the pigeon who spawned my errand.
Now the black-owned dry cleaners inflates in my sight line.
The owner's face zig-zagged with wrinkles. Her husband pops
his violet gum. Her husband pushes your body through his pin
machine. You, felt bolt, return in a wearable shape.

Here, the apron of felt, the edges sealed with fire from his gold
flip lighter. Here the gumball machine, no fee. And here, now,
come the double-dutch assassins—a fleet of all-ages troopers on
white stockinged feet. Here they come to block the gumball
machine. They are dressed like a drill team. Here come the
telephone cords pit-patting on the blacktop. *Jump in*, the
ropes *beg, jump in and get whipped. Your feet were never fleet and*
you'll get beaten in the street.

I evade the double-dutch assassins, but my every step a step on glass. My hair regrows its barrettes, retwists itself. I lose only one barrette, of plastic seafoam. (Long ago, I would have been punished for such loss as was the culture of the barrette.) Look here and you'll see me and shadow Shalimar running towards or away from a plaster church. Wearing the garments passed out for our assignment: white tights, white knit ponchos; hand-me-down prairie dresses with aprons and piping.

Here in our white patent leather mary janes. We're dressed very much the same. We are compact swarms of taffeta. We are ten fuzzy braids. A troupe composed of our doppelgängers murmur to score our lives. The murmur choir wears the double-dutch assassins' uniform: sashes of pink, gray, and emerald. They interject with step routines I cannot manage. Their skirts are magenta ankara. They don't have chants but sing the Negro National Anthem from memory.

When I jump, I cannot jump in. When I jump, the cord hits my ankles. When I jump, the ground hisses at the rope's slap in the disappointed hands of the double-dutch assassin, who also hisses. The ropes all limp as a beauty store snatchback under untrained fingers. The ropes fall limp as a father under a hot gun in the middle of the night. One looks toward others from the back of the formation. She raises her hand to greet me, my former doppelgänger. I tighten my white felt apron for a fight.

DOPPELGÄNGER:
You may, if you wish, have one more try, and then our bet is done. All of us are fleet of foot, you need jump only one.

After her rhyme, she checks with her compatriots, who suck their teeth at the delay. *But hurry up,* she relays for them, *Family Matters is on in fourty minutes.* Ok, that's fair. I jump. I land between the slack cords, lost as ever. Fearing justice, by which I mean rejection, remembering all the other times when I had failed alike. Waiting for their laughter, a fool in my outfit.

Now how will I be isolated? Who will make me their scapegoat? Their proxy for evil? Associate me with those who lurk obscured by shadow? Who will shape me as their fallen or their savior? *Oh, that. I'm sure you'll think it up yourself. Go fill your apron with gumballs before they close the dry cleaners.* Can I still have gumballs, I beg. *Of course. Who said you couldn't?* I suppose I assumed I no longer deserved sweetness. I suppose I'm used to punishment. I suppose it doesn't matter.

The ends of my twists now loose, I stride into the dry cleaners. Still, I fill my lap with gumballs, each of them shouting to me, each of them know my name, and all plead to return to their globe. Each lavender gumball heavy in my apron as perfumed lead, and just as sweet. I sit, the chaste berry tree to my back, apron of white felt draped as best it can to cover me. I wait for the pigeon to find me and dole out what I am sure is coming. Revolted with myself, well-covered, I wait to be turned back.

Through the whir of the salt film coating my eyeball, I search the sky and the trees for the pigeon, certain his clean timbs would prove a beacon through the fog that congealed around me. Searchlight for me in the dark night, lighthouse in the fog of life spent waiting for the rod to welt. But no—the hawk swoops too low. But no—the owl's eyes split open, oozing death. But no—the blue jay, a predator, a bright corvid without the gift of prophecy, unwanted by the great mysteries.

Low swoops the raven, a god among winged things. Low swoops the raven, overturning all but one gumball, into the mud of the forest, smashed beneath my feet, consumed with lolling head back, with a hard beaked grin. Low swoops Shalimar, now the raven of prophecy, beloved by mystery, feared by men, asks, *Who are you now, unpunished? Who are you now that you have been spared the rod that insulted your skin? Who are you? Who are you now?*

So I explain to the bird that *I have nothing, not even my history. I have no one, not even my own family. I've been nowhere I care to remember. I live a life I long to forget. I have no man, not even the one I chose. I have no money, nor does anyone I know. My hairline is receding. I was never clever or cunning or strong. I have constructed my life for the eyes of better people. I do not long to live long. I am cursed by what I remember, and damned by all I forgot.* Prostrate below the apron, I wait for absolution.

From the rocks a shake; from the trees a bend with no breeze; from the rocks a strut; from the trees a saunter, a shimmy, a revivifying buzz; from the rocks a whistle—from the rocks and trees, a voice, a chorus, a harmony—*nothing that is to be had can be lost, nothing you can do but find again. What could it be that you're searching for, beloved? Is it love? That's the only thing to be found on this expanse of rock, softened by green. Mother love? Here they whisper here. I will be your mother. Listen.*

Trees: *I am your mother*. Stones: *You are my son, I am your mother*. Trees: *you are my son*. Stones: *I am your mother*. Trees: *I am your mother*. Stones: *I am the tree*. Trees: *I am the stone*. Trees: *We are you*. Stones: *You are your mother*. Trees: *We are your mother*. Stones: *We are you*. Trees: *We are, and so you are*. Stones: *You are we*. Trees: *All are one*. Stones: *All are one*. With the stars knitted in their silent song, I felt the only truth. Next, from jagged, improvised mouths, they issued this:

THIS PAGE LEFT INTENTIONALLY BLANK

And the ancient plane trees, born of the earth, younger than sharks, older still than I or you or war or sex parted their lips and sang a song they learned from the mysteries:

No one can predict the will of Eros
I do not regret loving you, I'm just
stanching the blood drawn from Love's barbed arrows.

I'll try, try again, though my hope narrows
from ocean to river, stream to trickle, with trust
that no one can predict the will of Eros.

We're wise to anticipate Love's perils,
we're nimble, strong, and still may be flushed
in unstanched blood drawn from Love's arrows.

We'll win at love, we cry, we beg, marrow
dug, bone snapped in two by the boot of lust—
no one can predict the will of Eros.

We'll rage, we'll fuck, we'll pile our barrows
with shit, and praise, and prayer, always—we must
stanch the bright flow drawn from Love's barbed arrows.

A dilemma born before the Pharaohs,
love's wheel spins us around until we're dust
No one can predict the will of Eros,
so we must stanch the flow from Love's arrows.

We cannot master love, but we can try,
instead of sitting on our hands nonplussed
by the atrophy, the perfumed white lie
that flakes our bond, that erodes love to rust.

The unavoidable plight of lovers
who make of their crude obsession a hell
Yet they are wiser still than the others
who spit on the heels of true love. To dwell

on love's flaws is a sin against Eros.
Nothing else moves itself. It cannot be
created, but nor can it die. Morose
are bachelors, cads, and those who from love flee.

No one can predict the will of Eros,
so we must stanch the flow from Love's arrows.

THIS PAGE LEFT INTENTIONALLY BLANK

Song swallowed back into the rings of their throats, the nightbird watches me. *And who are you now that you know the truth of love, its rectitude, its wages and its contours—malign and sublime? Do you know what you couldn't know with me? With the man you left to wait in the woods?* demanded the bird. I say little. I grow into a monument inscribed for silence. I drink silence and it refreshes itself. A fish mouth above the water. His wing grazes my eyes and all is stars, opalescent stars.

SHALIMAR

Listen, there is more to do. You must follow the moss to the witch. She will not hide from you. You'll know her by her smell. She will remind you of the antecedent of your knowing, the kind the trees offered, lowering their branches and embracing you.

Their branches lower once more, press me into their mossy side, the north. Or shrug once the heft of a rattling flock rises and glides away at dawn. Or warn my waist against pratfalls and guide me home. My fellow travelers.

After miles, after days: rose syrup, honeysuckle, and pine on the air. A prefab home, green and white, with dirt blown o'er the western corners. A nook of sprawled green. Soil circle for a driveway. Pavement stones from the oak to the door. A brook growing nosy in its leisure; a blessing of frogs or fish consuming our usual embarrassment of biting spiders. By the pavement were communion whites—here a square-heeled shoe, bowl-bleached tights, badge, slip, round lace veil in the dirt.

I scour my body for the key that knows this door as the brook watches, as it checks over my shoulder, mouth curved to me. My hands slide over my shoulders, my hips, my knees, my shoes. The brook slides over me, glint-touched, the breathable slime off a slug. I try the knob, which turns for me. Gold flake sequins down my fingers and the walls hum electric and I vibrate. I am blown from room to room into her kitchen. I am bloated with hopeful nostalgia. I welcome our reunion.

I open my mouth and the brook pours out. I scoop frogs and fish back into my hingeless maw. I gape. I snort, never drowning yet so full of water, so dry on the outside. Constipated, uncrying, doomed to bog with my emotions. And moving, toward the brown tweed couch I find I am too much a vessel to sit, too much liquid for holding in my skin, there is no cork that can keep me, no lid for the feeling. I catch staple turned spike on the floor. I slosh across the brown shag.

Drained and flat on my back, supported by peeling linoleum tiles, I flop onto my side to find the chipped table arranged. Any flour brushed clean. Unopened mail moved to the wing chair's arm. Air plump with pork fat. Ancient pots simmer on the stovetop, then empty into butter tubs and plastic bowls alike. I make the cornbread from the box suggestions. Boxes still lurk below the table, we squat on our heels in oaken chairs. The rice and peas and greens and bread ready at once for once.

We pray and eat together with our feet above the indoor bloom, knowing the year begins with us all together here. The door squeals open—the water returning Mema's whites. They coast in on the ankle-high flow. Clothes bone-dry, crisp folded. They leak sylvan perfume, hovering slightly above the couch cushions. Mema sets her fork down on the table. Mema walks to the arch of the door. She dresses with the help of a humble wave. Protected, protective, she stands over me.

With hands as the bark of a tree she slaps a salve into my face, as once she worked in vaseline cut with a splash of water on a snowy morning before she walked me to the bus stop. Though her visage is ephemeral, she is still herself, my great-grandmother, sitting behind an apple pie, in her apron, her housecoat, surrounded by the yield of her garden.

MEMA:

I'm glad you're back. Let's get to work. Tell me what you believe you need if you are to survive—

Rose like a round emotion. Elusive among a loose webbing of possible injury. The risks we take for love are love. To be soft, to be defended in your smoothness—a towering aspiration, a need made true in the rose. A breath stands guard all night. A death that brings another harvest for birds and deer. A beauty creating its own respect. The red legend. The pink lover. The white ingénue. The blood mark of coming war scribed across chests of warriors, embroidered where the point will pierce.

Lily of the valley, a protector of the heart lost among the cast offs of man's medicine; always seeking to unseat the other, consume her sacred poisons, then rebrand them, patent them, and change their name to money. Holy to the ones who started the shift from granny midwife to a man in a cold white room, from wise women's wisdom to whatever we have now. Ripping us one system at a time. Was the foxglove worth what it reaped? Will we ever drink our lady's tears again?

Honeysuckle is April candy, a wet pleasure stolen from the verdant brush. A bump of childhood risking skunks, brambles, spiders, and the chastisement of streetlights alike for the aroma. The tongue thanks the dewdrop into dreams that appear in the daylight. The cream and gold unstoppable. The fragile prolific. But when it's time to trip, honeysuckle will tie for you. And when it's time to tip a little trap, it'll do for you. A tripwire, not a wall.

The mulberry bush by the valley where the car parts piled up from crashes. You were morbid—(Do you remember? Are there memories in this form?)—you'd hear the bend of metal and tip your way to see until the ambulance shouted its too late drawl. We only ate from the mulberry bush once, it had seen too much. Our small hands were scraped to bleeding on the brambles with a pinch worth of black sweet and a sad mouth of green sour, points sharp against our curious skin.

Always a pot of aloe by the hens & chickens in north light of the kitchen window. That's who you were, did you know? You were someone who could make anything grow. Aloe grew under your hand in the dark. Whether cut, or burn, or a chap from the bleach Aunt Ruby used for ringworm on my scalp. (No, the hair never grew back. Patch still blank as a brick.) The gel ran. You'd pinch the edge, wrap it in foil, use it until it was gone. (You're not truly gone.)

Yucca the crest on our phantom family flag. Yucca too deep in the yard to uproot, sprawling and spangled with beatles inside a copse of baby oaks. Three in a row. I know now how they make their soap, but I'll never know how they survived the floods we fled from. I'm sure the new resident will tear it from its perch and toss it on a heap to be carted away. I'm sure he doesn't care about their soap, or your care, or the garden once laid there. Its death is just space for some other american life.

Grapes, just like Great-Great-Grandma's homestead held—the arbor of grapes. The tire swing always so full of water. Aunt Gloria, steward of all things, in her slacks and Mack Truck bulldog hat. Alone in that house when her mother died but for the grapes and two men. She counted her days by packs of Camel filterless and those pinprick wine grapes wasped and raisined on the vine once she went blind. In that cloud of smoke she outlived all but one sister.

Mema laughs, mouth wide, dentures clucking in her softened face. Then the peal of my mother's easy giggle: the laughter of her surveillance at my recitation of whatever I had learned on their laps. My mother laughs, her face full of sour candy, fixated on the TV's specters. My mother at her long gone best. Asar lays, not quite opaque, where the gravel path meets the dirt of our backyard, his every breath an effort bearing its own rattle. I look toward the house where I thought I'd left him.

As I move closer, so built the heat off his skin. I respond with a sympathetic sweat, the unthinking reach to dab his brow. I wring out whatever water is left in me with lips twisted down. I scoop him and his heaving chest into my arms, recalling how slight a weight can be when split with the mind, duty a sort of strength. I lift and carry him, as I have done before, although he'd hate for me to tell you so, and as I did before, I carry him in the midst of a dangerous circumstance.

With time the fever does not break, the struggling chest never easing. I slit the boxes that hauled my jars from there to here, the little of what's left. I lament my tendency to leave tincture bottles unmarked, until a humble voice emerges—hum of words from the bleeding dandelion, how I remember my name. I scour the yard for half its yellow heads and roots. I scrub them to the sound of the stranger's footfalls, decocting them into a brew to try when none else can or will.

By morning, when the fever cools, I fall asleep in dawn's mild light, expecting a victory of trumpet flowers to greet my dreams but instead, a catastrophe—a still harder time before me—visions of war—a copse of churning bodies now useless to their owners, starved of their might but no threat in sight around me. So I lay down flat at a river bank and feel the armies inside of my stomach, feel the fear of their arrival at my neck, feel unready to play a role I still didn't know as I awake.

In the distance, feet. Drums. Tambourine. Shouts. Hollers. Cries for help. In the distance. Gunshots. The twisting of metal and the pop of rent flesh. The smell of rent flesh. A burning smell and a burning coming closer. A bloody smell approaching. The war slinks in on its belly ever nearer to us. It is pleased to arrive. Pissing on the singing trees. It reminds each of their lowly actions. Cutting low the horizon into a tableau without mercy. Who are you now? asks the war.

Old Familiar

When Watchnight breaks and we're still all together.
When the cobweb's shadow is sucked from the corners
of last year and the house glossed in easy tomorrows
we eat and we become a single thing. Forgetting the turn
of the card, so far behind us as to be before us again,
tonight we will make new promises, make love all night

then lose our tempers, drink to sway, fuck all night
and not be sweet about it neither. Just to be together.
And if this one texts an ex, or falls off the wagon again,
if we forget the slip of your sweet in light of your corners
it's no such thing. We'll come back to love. We'll turn
to you and listen to your song tonight, and tomorrow

we'll find a way to retire the habit. Apologize tomorrow
and so sincerely as to flush the hurt. We people of night
runs to wood panel liquor stores, people of been turned
out experience, people of sweat, people of put together
then disheveled come morning. Joy dotting each corner
as we walk home in or with our finest. Next year, again.

Next year, I'll plant the special morning glories, drip again
in a once weed-owned stamp of dirt, save seed for tomorrow
in smug assumption it will come (and it *will* come.) Corners
pressing out the old ways, evil or divine, multiplying like night
across the meridian. The sap that snaps us each together?
The vast drumbeat of gravity that hems up each of us in turn?

Next year, we'll learn to ride it. In our stirrups, ankles turning
steer us past the futile present. So what you got drunk again,
next year we'll meet up after the meetings, work it out together.
We are your community. We love you. Call me late tomorrow.
or whenever. I know that the hardest part can be the nights.
Maybe you don't feel it yet, but I think you turned the corner.

Hark, The New Year! In sequins! Ringing her bell in the corner
of the sweat-fogged room! The clock hands kiss, you turn
to face me, your lips a blush across my neck until the night
answers twilight's questions, then snore in wait of night again.
Might as well sleep. You'll head to work at dawn tomorrow.
I'll watch your eyes flicker in the cold room. Let's stay together.

I wasn't sure but now I'm certain. I see and love your corners.
Thank you for spending New Years with my people, their skin turn
glow in faint street light. My people, whose glory rivals the night.

Acknowledgments

Thank you to my grandmother, Barbara L. Johnson, who taught me art was both ritual and miracle. Thank you to my great-grandmother, Ruth Greene who taught me many things without talking often at all. Thank you to the Woodings, the Jennings, the Salters, and the Titus family. Thank you to the Hairston clan. Thank you to those I cannot name to thank.

Thank you to JD Stokely, Zefyr Lisowski, Leah Lakshmi Piepzna-Samarasinha, Alice Sheppard, Constantina Zavitsanos, and Josephine Shokrian for providing feedback on early versions of this work. Thank you to Major Jackson, Alice Quinn, and Dorothea Lasky for providing feedback on "psychedelia" when it was my MFA thesis at Columbia University.

Thank you to Lindsey Boldt and Jaye Elizabeth Elijah for editing this book, and Stephen Motika at Nightboat Books for publishing it. Thank you to Patty Berne and the Sins Invalid team for being flexible with me as I finished this book. Thank you to Empress Karen Rose and Sacred Vibes Apothecary.

Thank you to Sit + Write, without which I would have lagged in completing this work more frequently than I did. Thank you to Roots & River so long ago, who shaped what my work would become and define the tactics I employ to accomplish it. Thank you to the Oakland Queer and Trans People of Color Writer's Group, though decades defunct, for listening to me and allowing me to listen.

Thank you to bell hooks, whose feminist works on Blackness and gender helped shape my politics. Thank you to Toni Morrison, for *Song of Solomon* from which the name Shalimar emerged in this work. Again to my dear friends, occasional collaborators, and fellow travelers JD Stokely and Petra Floyd for creating their Shalimar, who is in conversation with my Shalimar. Thank you to Gil Scott-Heron whose question "who will survive in America?" spurred some of the inquiries contained in *WATCHNIGHT*.

Thank you to Prompt Press and Atmos who published early versions of "psychedelia" and "Sixth International" respectively. Thank you to *Guernica Magazine*, who published "Peach" and *The Yale Review*, who published "Requiem."

Thank you to Poetry Foundation for their financial support as I completed parts of this work. This project is supported in part by an award from the National Endowment for the Arts.

Cyrée Jarelle Johnson is a poet from Piscataway, New Jersey. He is also the author of *SLINGSHOT*, winner of a Lambda Literary Award for Gay Poetry. Johnson was awarded a Ruth Lilly and Dorothy Sargent Rosenberg Poetry Fellowship from the Poetry Foundation and served as the inaugural poet-in-residence at the Brooklyn Public Library. He is a 2023 National Endowment of the Arts Creative Writing Fellow.

NIGHTBOAT BOOKS

Nightboat Books, a nonprofit organization, seeks to develop audiences for writers whose work resists convention and transcends boundaries. We publish books rich with poignancy, intelligence, and risk. Please visit nightboat.org to learn about our titles and how you can support our future publications.

The following individuals have supported the publication of this book. We thank them for their generosity and commitment to the mission of Nightboat Books:

Kazim Ali
Anonymous (4)
Abraham Avnisan
Jean C. Ballantyne
The Robert C. Brooks Revocable Trust
Amanda Greenberger
Rachel Lithgow
Anne Marie Macari
Elizabeth Madans
Elizabeth Motika
Thomas Shardlow
Benjamin Taylor
Jerrie Whitfield & Richard Motika

This book is made possible, in part, by grants from the New York City Department of Cultural Affairs in partnership with the City Council, the New York State Council on the Arts Literature Program, and the National Endowment for the Arts.